Chicken Essentials

A Chicken Cookbook with Delicious Chicken Recipes

By
BookSumo Press
All rights reserved

Published by
http://www.booksumo.com

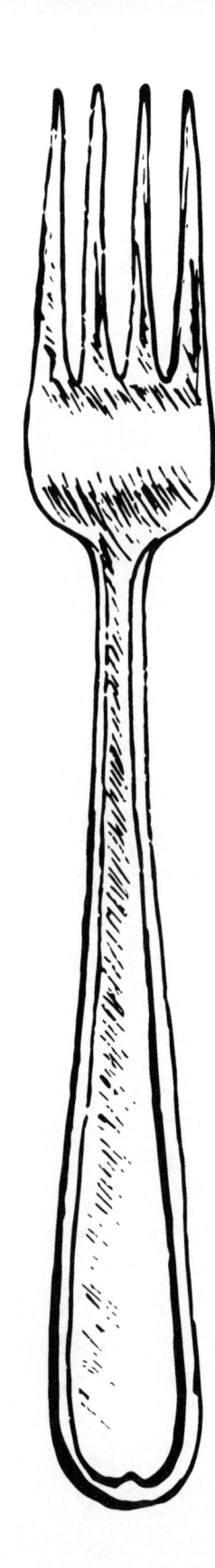

Table of Contents

Cilantro Dijon Chicken Cutlets 7

Maria's 6-ingredient Chili 8

Quesadillas Sedona 9

Sweet & Spicy Mustard Chicken Thighs 10

Carolinian Chicken 11

Fried Chicken South Carolina Style 12

BBQ Chicken Southern Style 14

Grandma's Baked Chicken 15

Chicken and Rice Carolina Style 16

Chicken Wings and Hot Sauce 17

Northern California Summer Mint Curry 18

Kathy's American Curried Chicken 20

Apple Quinoa Curry 21

Little Bay Yellow Curry 22

Chennai Inspired Chicken 23

Jamaican Curry Chicken I 24

Jamaican Curry Chicken II 25

Beginners' Creamy Chicken Stir Fry 26

Italian Bell Chicken Stir Fry 27

Oriental Chili Chicken and Ramen Stir Fry 28

Corny Grilled Chicken Stir Fry 29

Peanut Butter Chicken Stir Fry 30

A Texas-Mexican Stir Fry 31

Parsi Style Chicken Curry 32

East-Indian Chicken 34

Maple Syrup and Pecans Chicken Breast 35

Easy Backroad Style Chicken 36

Stuffed Chicken Breast VIII 37

Buttery Capers and Lemon Chicken 38

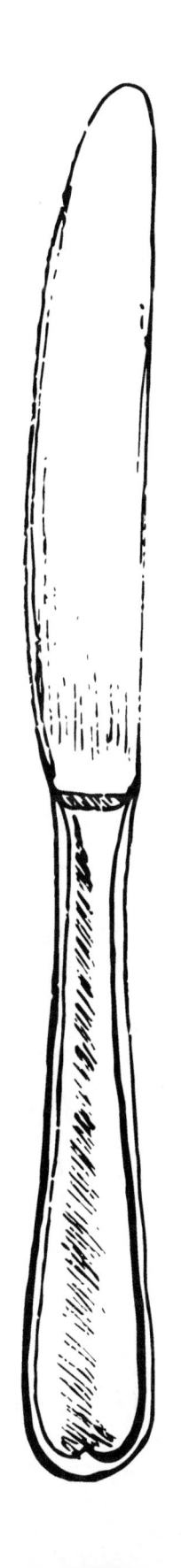

Buttermilk and Honey Chicken 39

Restaurant Style Chicken II 40

Artisan Style Chicken with Artichokes 41

Chicken Chili II 42

Goat Cheese and Balsamic Chicken Breast 43

Creole Style Chicken I 44

Thai Style Chicken III 45

Chili Peppers and Monterey Chicken 46

Vinegar and Salt Chicken 47

Arabic Style Chicken 48

Parsley, Peppers, and Sweet Onions Chicken 49

African Style Chicken 50

Japanese Style Chicken III 51

Cranberries and Onions Chicken 52

Creamy Chipotle Chicken 53

Sweet & Spicy Mustard Chicken Thighs 54

Chicken in Chipotle Gravy 55

Creamy Chipotle Chicken Sandwich 56

Rosa's Latin Chowder 57

Chicken Chowder for Champions 58

Grocery Store Rotisserie Chowder 59

How to Roast a Chicken 60

Fall-Spice Chicken Roast 61

4-Ingredient Chicken Roast 62

Southern Italian Chicken Roast 63

Herbs Marinade for Chicken Roast 64

Mediterranean Chicken Legs 65

Greek Inspired Chicken Roast 66

Glazed Chicken Roast 67

Orangy Baked Chicken 68

Baked Golden Chicken and Potato 69

Country Chicken Roast Gravy 70

Hot and Sweet Chicken Roast 71

Cilantro Dijon Chicken Cutlets

Prep Time: 10 mins
Total Time: 30 mins

Servings per Recipe: 4
Calories 173.0
Fat 6.1g
Cholesterol 83.1mg
Sodium 399.1mg
Carbohydrates 2.8g
Protein 25.7g

Ingredients

4 boneless skinless chicken breast halves
1 tbsp Dijon mustard
1 tbsp butter
1/2 C. prepared salsa
2 tbsp fresh lime juice
1/4 C. chopped fresh cilantro

Directions

1. Arrange each chicken breast between 2 plastic wrap sheets and with a meat mallet, pound into 1/2-inch thickness.
2. Spread mustard over each breast.
3. In a large skillet, melt the butter on medium heat and cook the chicken for about 3-4 minutes per side.
4. Stir in the salsa and lime juice and simmer, uncovered for about 6-8 minutes.
5. Serve with a sprinkling of the cilantro.

MARIA'S
6-ingredient Chili

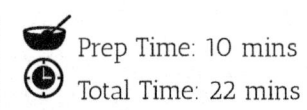

Prep Time: 10 mins
Total Time: 22 mins

Servings per Recipe: 4
Calories   328.6
Fat   4.8g
Cholesterol   56.6mg
Sodium   142.8mg
Carbohydrates   45.5g
Protein   30.4g

Ingredients

3 boneless skinless chicken breasts
1 (14 1/2 oz.) cans diced tomatoes (with peppers and onions)
1 tbsp chili powder
1 (15 oz.) cans black beans, drained and rinsed
1 (15 oz.) cans corn, drained
1/4 C. fresh cilantro, chopped

Directions

1. Cut the chicken into 1/2-inch chunks.
2. In a medium pan, mix together the chicken, undrained tomatoes and chili powder on medium heat and cook for about 5 minutes.
3. Add the remaining ingredients and simmer for about 5-7 minutes.

Quesadillas Sedona

🥣 Prep Time: 25 mins
⏱ Total Time: 55 mins

Servings per Recipe: 4
Calories   673 kcal
Fat   29.1 g
Carbohydrates   72.8g
Protein   31 g
Cholesterol   65 mg
Sodium   979 mg

Ingredients

- 2 tomatoes, diced
- 1 onion, finely chopped
- 2 limes, juiced
- 2 tbsp chopped fresh cilantro
- 1 jalapeño pepper, seeded and minced
- salt and pepper to taste
- 2 tbsp olive oil, divided
- 2 skinless, boneless chicken breast halves - cut into strips
- 1/2 onion, thinly sliced
- 1 green bell pepper, thinly sliced
- 2 cloves garlic, minced
- 4 (12 inch) flour tortillas
- 1 C. shredded Monterey Jack cheese
- 1/4 C. sour cream, for topping

Directions

1. In a small bowl, mix together the tomatoes, onion, lime juice, cilantro, jalapeño pepper, salt and pepper.
2. In a large skillet, heat 1 tbsp of the olive oil and sear the chicken till cooked through.
3. Transfer the chicken into a plate and keep aside.
4. In the same skillet, heat the remaining 1 tbsp of the olive oil and sauté the sliced onion and green pepper till tender. Stir in the minced garlic and sauté till aromatic.
5. Stir in half of the pico de gallo and cooked chicken.
6. Keep aside, covered to keep the mixture warm.
7. In a heavy skillet, heat 1 flour tortilla.
8. Spread 1/4 C. of the shredded cheese over the tortilla, followed by 1/2 of the chicken mixture and 1/4 C. of the cheese. Cover with another tortilla.
9. Cook till the bottom of tortillas becomes golden brown from both sides.
10. Remove the quesadilla from the skillet and cut into quarters.
11. Repeat with the remaining tortillas and filling.
12. Serve quesadillas with the sour cream and remaining pico de gallo.

SWEET & SPICY
Mustard Chicken Thighs

Prep Time: 20 mins
Total Time: 5 hrs

Servings per Recipe: 8
Calories   352 kcal
Fat   19 g
Carbohydrates   13.8g
Protein   29.1 g
Cholesterol   106 mg
Sodium   765 mg

Ingredients

8 large bone-in, skin-on chicken thighs
1/2 C. Dijon mustard
1/4 C. packed brown sugar
1/4 C. apple cider vinegar
1 tsp dry mustard powder
1 tsp salt
1 tsp freshly ground black pepper
1/2 tsp ground dried chipotle pepper
1 pinch cayenne pepper, or to taste
4 cloves garlic, minced
1 onion, sliced into rings
2 tsps vegetable oil, or as needed

Directions

1. With a sharp knife, cut 2 (1-inch apart) slashes into the skin and meat to the bone of the chicken thighs crosswise.
2. In a large bowl, mix together all the ingredients except onion and oil and transfer the mixture into a large resealable bag.
3. Add the chicken thighs and shake the bag to coat with marinade evenly and seal the bag tightly.
4. Refrigerate to marinate for about 4-8 hours.
5. Set your oven to 450 degrees F before doing anything else and line a large baking sheet with a lightly greased piece of foil.
6. Spread the onion rings onto the prepared baking sheet evenly and top with chicken thighs.
7. Coat the thighs with oil and sprinkle with seasoning if you like.
8. Cook in the oven for about 35-45 minutes or till done completely.
9. In a large serving platter, place thighs and onion rings.
10. In a small pan, add the baking sheet drippings and cook, stirring occasionally for about 3-4 minutes or till it reduces to half.
11. Serve the chicken and onion rings with the topping of pan sauce.

Carolinian Chicken

Prep Time: 30 mins
Total Time: 2 hrs

Servings per Recipe: 6
Calories	726 kcal
Fat	43 g
Carbohydrates	29.8g
Protein	50.9 g
Cholesterol	198 mg
Sodium	2756 mg

Ingredients

- 6 C. water
- 1 tbsp salt
- 1 onion, chopped
- 1 (3 lb.) whole chicken
- 3 1/2 C. chicken broth
- 1 C. long-grain white rice
- 1/2 lb. smoked beef sausage of your choice, sliced
- 2 tbsp Italian-style seasoning
- 2 cubes chicken bouillon

Directions

1. In a large pan, add the water, salt, onion and chicken and bring to a boil.
2. Cook for about 1 hour.
3. Transfer the chicken into a plate and keep aside to cool.
4. Remove the skin and bones of the chicken.
5. Chop the remaining meat into bite size pieces.
6. With a slotted spoon, skim off the fat from the chicken broth.
7. In a 6-quart pan, add about 3 1/2 C. of the chicken broth, rice, chicken pieces, sausage, herb seasoning and bouillon and cook for about 30 minutes.
8. Reduce the heat to low and simmer, covered till the desired consistency, stirring occasionally.

FRIED CHICKEN
South Carolina Style

🥣 Prep Time: 1 hr
🕐 Total Time: 1 hr

Servings per Recipe: 6
Calories 1445.6
Fat 70.5g
Cholesterol 366.7mg
Sodium 903.9mg
Carbohydrates 108.7g
Protein 87.7g

Ingredients

1 quart whole milk
kosher salt
1/2 C. sugar
2 (4 lb) roasting chickens, each cut into 8 pieces
2 C. buttermilk
2 large eggs, lightly beaten
1 tsp sweet paprika
1 tsp hot sauce
1/2 tsp fresh ground pepper
2 tsp baking powder
1 1/2 tsp baking soda
5 C. all-purpose flour
vegetable oil, for frying

Directions

1. In a small pan, mix together 1 C. of the milk, 3/4 C. of the kosher salt and sugar on medium heat and cook for about 2 minutes, stirring continuously.
2. Transfer the mixture into a large, deep bowl.
3. Add the remaining 3 C. of the milk and chicken pieces and stir to combine.
4. Refrigerate for about 4 hours.
5. Drain the chicken and rinse under the cold running water.
6. With the paper towels, pat dry the chicken pieces completely.
7. In a bowl, add the buttermilk, eggs, 1 tbsp of the kosher salt, paprika, hot sauce, pepper, baking powder and baking soda and mix till well combined.
8. In a large bowl, place the flour.
9. Coat the chicken pieces with the flour, tapping off any excess.
10. Dip the chicken pieces in the buttermilk mixture, letting the excess drip off.
11. Place the chicken pieces into the bowl of the flour and turn to coat.

12. In a large, deep skillet, heat the oil on medium heat and cook the chicken pieces, covered for about 5 minutes.
13. Uncover and cook for about 18-20 minutes, flipping occasionally.
14. Transfer the chicken pieces onto the paper towel lined plate to drain.
15. Serve hot or warm.

BBQ CHICKEN
Southern Style

Prep Time: 15 mins
Total Time: 35 mins

Servings per Recipe: 8
Calories	655.9
Fat	30.1g
Cholesterol	108.9mg
Sodium	693.8mg
Carbohydrates	56.3g
Protein	37.2g

Ingredients

3/4 C. molasses
1/2 C. pure olive oil
1/2 C. chicken broth
2 tbsp Dijon mustard
2 tbsp soy sauce
2 tbsp fresh ground pepper
1 tbsp Worcestershire sauce
1 shallot, minced
1 green onion, chopped
3 lbs chicken breasts, thighs, quarters, drumsticks, bone in

BBQ Sauce:
2 C. yellow mustard
3/4 C. light brown sugar
1/4 C. strong brewed coffee
2 tbsp honey
1 tbsp molasses
1 tbsp liquid smoke
2 tsp Worcestershire sauce
2 tsp Tabasco sauce

Directions

1. For the sauce in a medium pan, mix together all the ingredients and bring to a gentle boil.
2. Stir well and remove from the heat.
3. Keep aside in the room temperature to cool.
4. After cooling, transfer into a glass jar with lid and refrigerate.
5. For the chicken in a large bowl, add all the ingredients except chicken and mix well.
6. Keep aside in the room temperature for about 30 minutes.
7. Add the chicken pieces and coat with the mixture generously.
8. Refrigerate for overnight.
9. Set the broiler of your oven and arrange oven rack about 12-inch from the heating element.
10. Remove the chicken from the marinade and arrange the pieces onto a large baking sheet.
11. coat the chicken pieces with the barbecue sauce and cook under the broiler for about 8-10 minutes per side, flipping occasionally and rotating.

Grandma's Baked Chicken

Prep Time: 10 mins
Total Time: 1 hr 15 mins

Servings per Recipe: 4
Calories 944.3
Fat 63.3g
Cholesterol 297.9mg
Sodium 431.8mg
Carbohydrates 15.8g
Protein 74.3g

Ingredients

- 1 (3 1/2-4 lb) broiler-fryer chickens
- 1 sweet onion, cut into large chunks
- 1 small apple, unpeeled and cut into large chunks
- 2 small celery ribs
- fresh herb
- salt
- freshly grated black pepper
- Glaze:
- 1 tbsp oil
- 2 tbsp apple juice
- 2 tbsp honey
- 1 tbsp lime juice
- 1/2 tsp paprika
- 1/4 tsp sea salt

Directions

1. Set your oven to 325 degrees F before doing anything else and arrange a rack in a large roasting pan.
2. Wash the chicken and with the paper towels, pat dry.
3. Season the cavity of the chicken with the salt and pepper.
4. Stuff the cavity with the onion, apple and celery and with the cooking string, tie the legs.
5. For the glaze in a small bowl, mix together all the ingredients.
6. Rub the whole chicken with a small amount of the glaze evenly.
7. Reserve the remaining glaze.
8. Arrange the chicken over the rack in roasting pan and cook in the oven for about 2 hours, basting with the glaze and pan juices after every 20-30 minutes.
9. Remove from the oven and with a piece of the foil, cover the chicken and keep aside for about 10-15 minutes before carving.

CHICKEN and Rice Carolina Style

Prep Time: 10 mins
Total Time: 50 mins

Servings per Recipe: 10
Calories 509.6
Fat 30.0g
Cholesterol 92.1mg
Sodium 665.7mg
Carbohydrates 31.2g
Protein 25.8g

Ingredients

12 oz. turkey bacon, chopped
2 C. long-grain rice
4 C. chicken broth, boiling
1 whole chicken, cut up (3 1/2 lb.)
4 stalks celery, cut into 1 inch pieces
1 carrot, cut in 1 inch pieces

1 bay leaf
salt and pepper
2 tbsp fresh parsley, chopped

Directions

1. Heat a large skillet and cook the bacon on very low heat till crisp.
2. Transfer the bacon onto a paper towel lined plate to drain and then crumble it.
3. Drain the grease, leaving 2 tbsp inside the skillet.
4. In the same skillet, add the rice and cook slowly till browned lightly.
5. Stir in the boiling stock and bring back to a boil.
6. Stir in the chicken, vegetables, bay leaf, salt and pepper.
7. Reduce the heat and simmer, covered for about 30 minutes.
8. Serve hot with a sprinkling of the crumbled bacon and parsley.

Chicken Wings and Hot Sauce

Prep Time: 30 mins
Total Time: 45 mins

Servings per Recipe: 4
Calories   1231 kcal
Fat   116.7 g
Carbohydrates   3.1g
Protein   44.2 g
Cholesterol   161 mg
Sodium   980 mg

Ingredients

- 1 gallon peanut oil
- 25 chicken wings, segmented and patted dry with paper towels
- 1/3 C. unsalted butter, melted
- 1/2 C. hot pepper sauce
- 1 tbsp garlic powder
- 1 tbsp coarse-ground black pepper

Directions

1. In a deep-fryer, heat the oil to 375 degrees F.
2. Gently add the wings, one at a time, to the hot oil and gently fry for about 15 minutes.
3. In a large bowl, add the the melted butter, hot pepper sauce, garlic powder and black pepper and mix till well combined.
4. Add the cooked wings and turn to coat.
5. Serve immediately.

NORTHERN CALIFORNIA
Summer Mint Curry

Prep Time: 1 hr
Total Time: 3 hrs 45 mins

Servings per Recipe: 8
Calories	552 kcal
Fat	38.4 g
Carbohydrates	28.9 g
Protein	28.9 g
Cholesterol	59 mg
Sodium	612 mg

Ingredients

1/2 C. dried red chili peppers, stems and seeds removed
1/2 C. boiling water
2 C. grated fresh coconut
2 tbsps ground coriander
2 tbsps ground cumin
2 tbsps fennel seeds
1/4 C. peanut oil, divided
1/3 C. sliced almonds
5 stalks lemon grass, trimmed and thinly sliced
1 whole head garlic, cloves peeled and crushed
1/2 C. peeled and diced fresh ginger root
3 (1 1/2 inch) pieces fresh turmeric root, peeled and roughly diced 5
shallots, peeled and roughly diced
water, or as needed
3 tbsps whole star anise pods
2 (2 inch) sticks cinnamon
2 tbsps whole cloves
2 tbsps whole cardamom pods
1/2 C. diced fresh mint, stems reserved
1/2 C. water
2 lbs boneless, skinless chicken breast halves, cubed
2 tsps kosher salt
1 (14 oz.) can coconut milk
1 lime, juiced
1 pinch kosher salt to taste

Directions

1. Let your chilies sit in boiling water (1/2 C.) for 40 mins. Then remove the liquids.
2. Begin to toast your coconut for 6 mins while stirring then place the coconut in a bowl.
3. Toast your fennel seeds, cumin, and coriander for 2 mins then place the toasted spices to the side.
4. Get your food processor and puree the following: fennel seeds, 2 tbsp peanut oil, cumin, toasted coconut, and coriander.
5. Once the mix is smooth add: turmeric, chili, ginger, almonds, shallots, garlic, and lemon grass.

6. Continue to puree everything to form a paste. Then add a tbsp of water or 2 if you would like to make the mix smoother.
7. Now add the rest of the peanut oil (2 tbsp) to a frying pan and being to get it hot. Add the mint stems, star anise, cardamom pods, cinnamon sticks and cloves to the oil.
8. Let the spice fry for 3 mins.
9. Now remove all the spices and throw them away.
10. Add the puree to the seasoned oil and cook the mix for 4 mins then add: 2 tsps kosher salt, 1/2 C. water, and the chicken.
11. Cook the chicken for about 12 mins until it is fully done then add in the coconut milk.
12. Get everything boiling and once the mix is boiling, set the heat to low, and let the mix gently cook for 75 mins.
13. Now add the lime juice, mint leaves, and some more salt.
14. Cook everything for 3 more mins.
15. Enjoy.

KATHY'S American Curried Chicken

Prep Time: 10 mins
Total Time: 1 hr 20 mins

Servings per Recipe: 18
Calories	315 kcal
Fat	17.7 g
Carbohydrates	17.4g
Protein	22.1 g
Cholesterol	86 mg
Sodium	210 mg

Ingredients

- 18 cut up chicken pieces
- 1/4 C. prepared mustard
- 1 C. honey
- 3 tbsp curry powder
- 2 (4.5 oz.) cans mushrooms, drained
- 1 (4.5 oz.) can mushrooms, drained, liquid reserved

Directions

1. Set your oven to 300 degrees F before doing anything else.
2. In a 13x9-inch baking dish, arrange the chicken pieces.
3. In a microwave safe bowl, mix together the mustard, honey and curry powder and microwave on High for about 1 minute.
4. Remove from the microwave and stir in the mushrooms.
5. Place the mushroom mixture over the chicken evenly.
6. Cook in the oven for about 45-50 minutes, flipping once after 30 minutes.

Apple Quinoa Curry

🥣 Prep Time: 30 mins
🕐 Total Time: 4 hrs 30 mins

Servings per Recipe: 6
Calories   185 kcal
Fat   3.1 g
Carbohydrates   14.4g
Protein   24.4 g
Cholesterol   59 mg
Sodium   75 mg

Ingredients

1 1/2 lb. diced chicken breast meat
3/4 C. chopped onion
1 1/4 C. chopped celery
1 3/4 C. chopped Granny Smith apples
1 C. chicken broth

1/4 C. nonfat milk
1 tbsp curry powder
1/4 tsp paprika
1/3 C. quinoa

Directions

1. In a slow cooker, add the chicken, onion, celery, apple, chicken broth, milk, curry powder and paprika and stir till well combined.
2. Set the slow cooker on Low and cook, covered for about 4-5 hours.
3. In the 35 minutes of the cooking, stir in the quinoa.
4. Serve hot.

LITTLE
Bay Yellow Curry

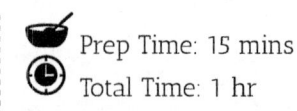

Prep Time: 15 mins
Total Time: 1 hr

Servings per Recipe: 4
Calories 412 kcal
Fat 30.7 g
Carbohydrates 11.9 g
Protein 26.3 g
Cholesterol 59 mg
Sodium 594 mg

Ingredients

2 tbsp vegetable oil
1 white onion, chopped
2 cloves garlic, crushed
1 lb. skinless, boneless chicken breast halves - chopped
1 small head cauliflower, chopped
2 1/2 tbsp yellow curry powder
1 tsp garlic salt
1 (14 oz.) can unsweetened coconut milk
1/3 C. chicken stock
salt and pepper to taste

Directions

1. In a large skillet, heat the oil on medium heat and sauté the onion and garlic till tender.
2. Stir in the chicken and cook for about 10 minutes.
3. Stir in the cauliflower, curry powder, garlic salt, coconut milk, chicken stock, salt and pepper.
4. Reduce the heat to low and simmer for about 30 minutes, stirring occasionally.

Chennai Inspired Chicken

Prep Time: 25 mins
Total Time: 1 d 45 mins

Servings per Recipe: 4
Calories   356 kcal
Fat   18.8 g
Carbohydrates   13.7g
Protein   35.6 g
Cholesterol   102 mg
Sodium   734 mg

Ingredients

- 2 lb. chicken, cut into pieces
- 1 tsp salt
- 1 lemon, juiced
- 1 1/4 C. plain yogurt
- 1/2 onion, finely chopped
- 1 clove garlic, minced
- 1 tsp grated fresh ginger root
- 2 tsp garam masala
- 1 tsp cayenne pepper
- 2 tsp finely chopped cilantro
- 1 lemon, cut into wedges

Directions

1. Remove the skin from the chicken pieces and with a sharp knife, cut slits into each piece lengthwise.
2. In a shallow dish, place the chicken pieces.
3. Sprinkle the chicken with the salt and drizzle with the lemon juice evenly.
4. Keep aside for about 20 minutes.
5. In a large bowl, add the yogurt, onion, garlic, ginger, garam masala and cayenne pepper and mix till smooth.
6. Add the chicken and coat with the yogurt mixture generously.
7. Refrigerate, covered for about 6 - 24 hours.
8. Set your outdoor grill for medium - high heat and lightly, grease the grill grate.
9. Cook the chicken on grill till done completely from both sides.
10. Serve with a garnishing of the cilantro and lemon wedges.

JAMAICAN
Curry Chicken I

Prep Time: 20 mins
Total Time: 50 mins

Servings per Recipe: 6
Calories	348 kcal
Carbohydrates	13.8 g
Cholesterol	103 mg
Fat	20.3 g
Protein	27.8 g
Sodium	1353 mg

Ingredients

1/4 C. curry powder, divided
2 tbsps garlic powder
1 tbsp seasoned salt
1 tbsp onion powder
2 tsps salt
1 sprig fresh thyme, leaves stripped
1 pinch ground allspice, or more to taste
salt and ground black pepper to taste
2 1/4 lbs whole chicken, cut into pieces
3 tbsps vegetable oil
3 C. water
1 potato, diced

1/2 C. chopped carrots
2 scallions (green onions), chopped
1 (1 inch) piece fresh ginger root, minced
1 Scotch bonnet chili pepper, chopped, or to taste

Directions

1. Get a bowl and combine the following: pepper, 2 tbsps curry, salt, garlic powder, allspice, seasoned salt, thyme, onion powder.
2. Cover your chicken with the dry seasoning evenly.
3. Get a frying pan. Get 2 tbsps of curry and oil hot. Heat for 2 mins.
4. Mix in in chicken. Set heat to medium and combine carrot, water, potato, chili pepper, ginger, and scallions.
5. Place a lid on pan and let chicken simmer for 40 mins. Temp should be 165 degrees. Set chicken aside. Let the gravy get thicker if you like, by continuing to heat, otherwise serve.
6. Enjoy.

Jamaican Curry Chicken II

Prep Time: 10 mins
Total Time: 55 mins

Servings per Recipe: 4
Calories	210 kcal
Carbohydrates	6.2 g
Cholesterol	30 mg
Fat	15.4 g
Protein	12.5 g
Sodium	322 mg

Ingredients

- 1/4 C. vegetable oil
- 1 onion, chopped
- 1 tomato, chopped
- 1 garlic clove, chopped
- 2 tbsps Jamaican-style curry powder, see appendix
- 2 slices habanero pepper (optional)
- 1/4 tsp ground thyme
- 2 skinless, boneless chicken breast halves, cut into 1 1/2-inch pieces
- 1 C. water
- 1/2 tsp salt, or to taste

Directions

1. Get a frying pan. Get veggie oil hot.
2. Stir fry habaneros, onion, thyme, tomato, curry powder, and garlic for 7 mins. Add chicken and fry for 5 mins.
3. Add water to the onions and chicken, and set heat to low. Place a lid on pan. Let everything lightly boil for 30 mins.
4. Enjoy.

BEGINNERS'
Creamy Chicken Stir Fry

Prep Time: 20 mins
Total Time: 1 hr 20 mins

Servings per Recipe: 4
Calories   305 kcal
Fat   17.5 g
Carbohydrates   8.3g
Protein   28.1 g
Cholesterol   96 mg
Sodium   1102 mg

Ingredients

1 lb skinless, boneless chicken breast halves, cut into bite size pieces
1/2 onion, chopped
1 green bell pepper, chopped
1/4 C. butter
1 tsp paprika

1 tsp garlic salt
seasoning salt to taste
1 (10.75 oz) can condensed cream of mushroom soup
1/2 C. water

Directions

1. Place a large pan or wok over low heat. Heat the butter in it until it melts. Add the chicken, onion and green bell pepper then cook them for 7 min.
2. Add the paprika garlic salt and seasoned salt. Put on the lid and cook them for 17 min. Stir in the water with soup and bring them to a simmer.
3. Cook the stir fry until it becomes thick. Serve it hot with some rice.
4. Enjoy.

Italian Bell Chicken Stir Fry

Prep Time: 15 mins
Total Time: 30 mins

Servings per Recipe: 4
Calories   210 kcal
Fat   7.9 g
Carbohydrates   10.2g
Protein   24.2 g
Cholesterol   59 mg
Sodium   297 mg

Ingredients

- 2 tbsp all-purpose flour
- 1 tsp garlic powder
- salt and pepper to taste
- 1 lb skinless, boneless chicken breast meat - cut into cubes
- 1 tsp vegetable oil
- 1 red bell pepper, sliced
- 1 small onion, chopped
- 1 C. sliced zucchini
- 1 C. sliced fresh mushrooms
- 1/4 C. chicken broth
- 1/4 C. Italian salad dressing

Directions

1. Get a zip lock bag: Combine in it the flour, garlic powder, salt, and pepper with chicken dices. Seal the bag and toss them to coat.
2. Place a large wok or pan over medium heat. Heat the oil in it. Cook in it the chicken dices for 7 min.
3. Add the bell pepper, onion, zucchini, mushrooms, chicken broth, and Italian dressing. Put on the lid and cook them for 12 min. Serve your stir fry hot with rice or noodles.
4. Enjoy.

ORIENTAL
Chili Chicken and Ramen Stir Fry

Prep Time: 15 mins
Total Time: 30 mins

Servings per Recipe: 2
Calories   438 kcal
Fat   14.1 g
Carbohydrates   47.6g
Protein   31.9 g
Cholesterol   65 mg
Sodium   1118 mg

Ingredients

1 1/2 C. hot water
1 (3 oz) package Oriental-flavor ramen noodle soup mix
2 tsp vegetable oil, divided
8 oz skinless, boneless chicken breast halves, cut into 2-inch strips
2 C. broccoli florets
1 C. sliced onion wedges
2 cloves garlic, minced
1 C. fresh bean sprouts
1/2 C. water
1/2 C. sliced water chestnuts
1 tsp soy sauce
1 tsp oyster sauce
1/4 tsp chile-garlic sauce (such as Sriracha(R)), or to taste
1 roma tomato, cut into wedges

Directions

1. Pour 1 1/2 C. of water in a heavy saucepan. Cook in it the noodles for 3 min. Remove it from the water and place it aside.
2. Place a large pan or wok over medium heat. Heat 1 tsp of oil in it. Add the chicken and cook it for 7 min. Drain the chicken and place it aside.
3. Turn the heat to high. Add the broccoli, onion, and garlic. Cook them for 7 min.
4. Stir in the ramen seasoning packet with noodles, bean sprouts, water, water chestnuts, soy sauce, oyster sauce, and chile-garlic sauce.
5. Cook them for 6 min. Stir in the tomato and cook them for 4 min. Serve your stir fry hot.
6. Enjoy.

Corny Grilled Chicken Stir Fry

Prep Time: 15 mins
Total Time: 35 mins

Servings per Recipe: 4
Calories   313 kcal
Fat   9.6 g
Carbohydrates   29.1g
Protein   25 g
Cholesterol   52 mg
Sodium   915 mg

Ingredients

- 3 skinless, boneless chicken breast halves - cut into strips
- 2 tbsp olive oil
- 1 onion, sliced
- 1 red bell pepper, seeded and cubed
- 1 yellow bell pepper, seeded and cubed
- 1 (15 oz) can baby corn, drained
- 1 tbsp white sugar
- 1 (16 oz) package frozen stir-fry vegetables
- 1 C. water
- 1 tbsp cornstarch
- 1 tbsp soy sauce

Directions

1. Before you do anything preheat the grill and grease it.
2. Cook the chicken strips in the grill for 8 min. Place them aside to lose heat completely. Cut them into dices.
3. Place a large pan or wok over medium heat. Heat the oil in it. Cook in it the onion for 3 min.
4. Stir in the red and yellow pepper, baby corn, and the stir-fry veggies. Turn the heat to high medium. Cook them for 17 min.
5. Get a small mixing bowl: Whisk in it the cornstarch with water.
6. Stir in the salt with chicken, sugar, soy sauce, and cornstarch mix. Cook them until the stir fry becomes thick. Serve it hot with some rice or noodles.
7. Enjoy.

PEANUT BUTTER
Chicken Stir Fry

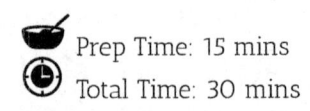

Prep Time: 15 mins
Total Time: 30 mins

Servings per Recipe: 4
Calories   344 kcal
Fat   16.6 g
Carbohydrates   24.4g
Protein   28 g
Cholesterol   54 mg
Sodium   412 mg

Ingredients

1/2 C. chicken broth
2 C. sliced mushrooms
1/2 sweet onion, sliced
1 small head broccoli, cut into spears
1 tbsp tamari or soy sauce
1/4 C. creamy peanut butter
1 pinch red pepper flakes (optional)
1 (12 oz) package shredded coleslaw mix

3 C. bean sprouts
1 (9 oz) package diced cooked chicken breast meat
1 tbsp toasted sesame seeds (optional)

Directions

1. Place a large pan over medium heat. Pour the broth in it. Cook it until it starts boiling.
2. Stir in the broccoli with onion and mushroom. Put on the lid and cook them for 6 min. Add the tamari, peanut butter, and pepper flakes. Mix them until they become smooth.
3. Stir in the coleslaw mix, bean sprouts, and chicken. Cook them for 4 min. Serve your stir fry hot.
4. Enjoy.

A Texas-Mexican Stir Fry

Prep Time: 20 mins
Total Time: 35 mins

Servings per Recipe: 4
Calories   333 kcal
Carbohydrates   13.3 g
Cholesterol   94 mg
Fat   5.9 g
Protein   32.1 g
Sodium   945 mg

Ingredients

- 1 tsp olive oil
- 1 green bell pepper, chopped
- 1 red bell pepper, chopped
- 2 tbsps all-purpose flour, or as needed
- 1 (1 ounce) packet taco seasoning mix
- 1 pound skinless, boneless chicken breast halves, diced
- 2 tsps olive oil
- 1 (15 ounce) can black beans, rinsed and drained
- 1/2 cup prepared salsa
- 1 cup shredded Cheddar cheese

Directions

1. Get a skillet, heat 1 tsp olive oil. Fry red and green peppers for 5 mins, remove them.
2. Grab a bowl combine the following: taco seasoning and flour. Add your chicken. Coat the chicken.
3. Get your wok. Heat 2 tsps of olive oil. Fry chicken for five mins, until cooked.
4. Combine the peppers from earlier with the chicken and also add some salsa, and black beans.
5. Stir fry, the chicken, the peppers, the beans, and salsa for 5 mins.
6. Serve with cheddar cheese.
7. Enjoy.

PARSI STYLE
Chicken Curry

Prep Time: 30 mins
Total Time: 1 hr 10 mins

Servings per Recipe: 4
Calories   649 kcal
Fat   23.1 g
Carbohydrates   75.3g
Protein   40.1 g
Cholesterol   117 mg
Sodium   168 mg

Ingredients

8 chicken drumsticks
salt and pepper to taste
2 tbsp olive oil
3 cloves garlic, minced
1/2 tsp red pepper flakes
4 C. apricot nectar
1 tsp cornstarch
1 tbsp water
3 tbsp Madras curry powder

1 C. dried apricots
1 large onion, roughly chopped
1 large green bell pepper, roughly chopped
4 carrots, thinly sliced
1 fresh green chili pepper, minced (optional)
1/2 C. chopped water chestnuts (optional)

Directions

1. Set your oven to 350 degrees F before doing anything else.
2. Season the chicken drumsticks with the salt and pepper.
3. In a large oven-safe skillet, heat the olive oil on medium heat and sauté the garlic and red pepper flakes for about 1-2 minutes.
4. Add the drumsticks and sear for about 3 minutes per side.
5. Transfer the skillet into the oven.
6. Cook in the oven for about 7-10 minutes.
7. In a large pan, add the apricot nectar and bring to a boil on medium-high heat.
8. Meanwhile, in a small bowl, dissolve the cornstarch in water.
9. Reduce the heat to medium-low and stir in the cornstarch mixture and curry powder.
10. Add the dried apricots and stir to combine.
11. Transfer the baked drumsticks into the apricot mixture and remove from the heat.
12. Heat the same skillet used to cook the chicken on medium heat and sauté the onion, green bell pepper, carrots and green chili pepper and cook till the onion becomes softened.

13. Add the drumsticks and apricot sauce and simmer, covered for about 10 minutes.
14. Season with the salt and pepper.
15. Stir in the water chestnuts and serve immediately.

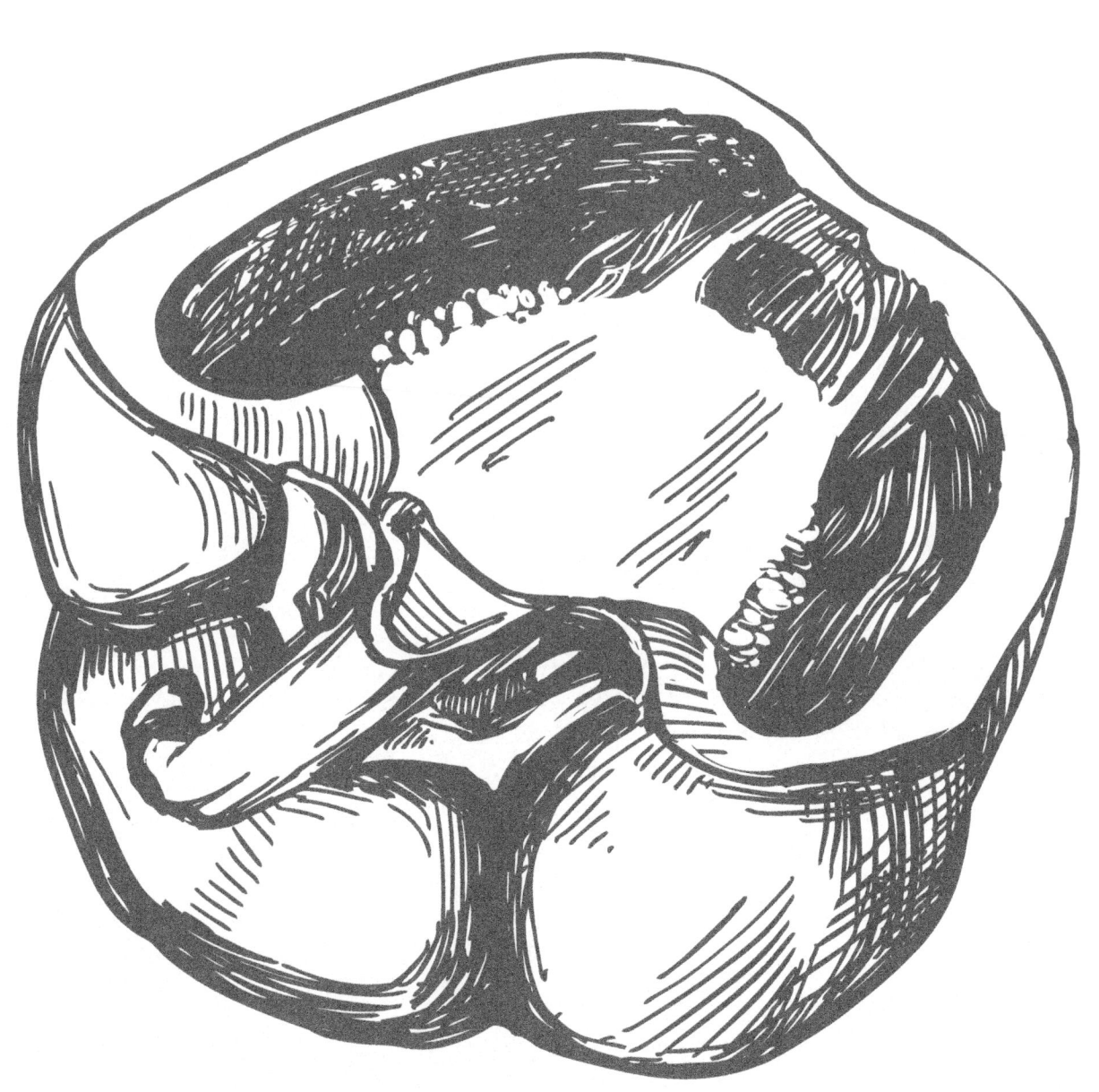

EAST-INDIAN
Chicken

Prep Time: 15 mins
Total Time: 40 mins

Servings per Recipe: 4
Calories   426 kcal
Fat   13 g
Carbohydrates   55.8g
Protein   24.9 g
Cholesterol   73 mg
Sodium   377 mg

Ingredients

1 lb. chicken tenders, cut into bite-size pieces
2 tsp garam masala
1 tsp garlic powder
salt and black pepper to taste
2 tbsp olive oil
1/2 yellow onion, finely diced
1 1/2 C. chicken stock
1 C. apricot preserves
1/4 C. white vinegar
1 tsp hot pepper sauce (such as Tabasco(R))
1 tsp lime zest
1 tbsp butter

Directions

1. Season the chicken with the garam masala, garlic powder, salt and pepper.
2. In a skillet, heat the olive oil on medium heat and sauté the onions for about 5 minutes.
3. Add the chicken and cook for about 5 minutes.
4. Transfer the chicken mixture into a bowl and keep aside.
5. In the same skillet, add 1 C. of the chicken stock and bring to a simmer, scraping the brown bits from the bottom of the skillet.
6. Stir in the apricot preserves, vinegar, remaining chicken stock and hot sauce.
7. Return the chicken mixture and simmer for about 10 minutes.
8. Stir in the lime zest and butter just before serving.

Maple Syrup and Pecans Chicken Breast

Prep Time: 10 mins
Total Time: 25 mins

Servings per Recipe: 4
Calories   447 kcal
Fat   30.3 g
Carbohydrates   15g
Protein   30.4 g
Cholesterol   84 mg
Sodium   700 mg

Ingredients

- 14 skinless, boneless chicken breasts
- 2 tbsps real maple syrup
- 1 C. chopped pecans
- 3 tbsps all-purpose flour
- 1 tsp salt
- 2 tbsps butter
- 1 tbsp vegetable oil

Directions

1. Get a bowl, combine: salt, flour, and pecans.
2. Coat your chicken pieces with syrup then cover each piece with the pecans.
3. Fry these chicken pieces in butter for 14 mins.
4. Enjoy with some cooked brown rice.

EASY Backroad Style Chicken

Prep Time: 10 mins
Total Time: 8 hrs 30 mins

Servings per Recipe: 4
Calories   676 kcal
Fat   57.4 g
Carbohydrates 19 g
Protein   23.3 g
Cholesterol   61 mg
Sodium   717 mg

Ingredients

4 skinless, boneless chicken breast halves
1 C. Worcestershire sauce
1 C. vegetable oil
1 C. lemon juice
1 tsp garlic powder

Directions

1. Get a bowl, combine: garlic, Worcestershire, lemon juice, and oil. Place a lid on the bowl, and marinate everything in the fridge overnight.
2. Turn on your oven's broiler and ensure that the grate is 6 inches away from the heating source.
3. Once the broiler is hot, broil your chicken for 8 mins per side until cooked fully.
4. Enjoy.

Stuffed Chicken Breast VIII (Apples and Cheddar)

Prep Time: 15 mins
Total Time: 40 mins

Servings per Recipe: 4
Calories   139 kcal
Fat   5.1 g
Carbohydrates   4.9g
Protein   15 g
Cholesterol   46 mg
Sodium   120 mg

Ingredients

- 2 skinless, boneless chicken breasts
- 1/2 C. chopped apple
- 2 tbsps shredded Cheddar cheese
- 1 tbsp Italian-style dried bread crumbs
- 1 tbsp butter
- 1/4 C. chicken broth
- 1/4 C. water
- 1 tbsp water
- 1 1/2 tsps cornstarch
- 1 tbsp chopped fresh parsley, for garnish

Directions

1. Get a bowl, mix: bread crumbs, cheese, and apples.
2. With a mallet pound out your chicken pieces, then add an equal amount of filling to the center of each.
3. Shape the chicken pieces into a roll and then stake a toothpick through each.
4. Sear your chicken in butter then once it is browned all over add your water and broth.
5. Place a lid on the pan and let the contents gently cook for 17 mins.
6. Place your chicken on a serving platter and then add some cornstarch and a tbsp of water to the remaining broth in the pot.
7. Heat and stir the cornstarch to form a gravy to top your chicken with.
8. Serve the chicken rolls with a topping of parsley and gravy.
9. Enjoy.

BUTTERY Capers and Lemon Chicken

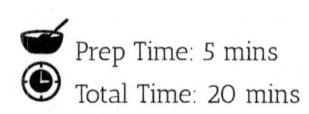

Prep Time: 5 mins
Total Time: 20 mins

Servings per Recipe: 4
Calories   313 kcal
Fat   21.2 g
Carbohydrates   1.8g
Protein   28.2 g
Cholesterol   132 mg
Sodium   974 mg

Ingredients

- 4 boneless, skinless chicken breast halves
- 1 tsp lemon pepper
- 1 tsp salt
- 1 tsp dried dill weed
- 1 tsp garlic powder
- 3 tbsps butter
- 1/2 C. whipping cream
- 2 tbsps capers, drained and rinsed

Directions

1. Coat your chicken with garlic powder, lemon pepper, dill, and salt. Then for 6 mins sear the chicken in butter making sure to turn the chicken repeatedly.
2. Set your heat to low and cook the contents for 8 mins until fully done.
3. Place your chicken to the side and wrap them with some foil.
4. In the same pan turn up the heat and add in whipping cream.
5. Cook the cream for 4 mins while stirring then add the capers.
6. Top the chicken with the cream and serve with some cooked angel hair pasta.
7. Enjoy.

Buttermilk and Honey Chicken

Prep Time: 10 mins
Total Time: 1 hr 45 mins

Servings per Recipe: 4
Calories   481 kcal
Fat   21.5 g
Carbohydrates   49.4g
Protein   22.8 g
Cholesterol   65 mg
Sodium   6378 mg

Ingredients

- 3 C. cold water
- 1/4 C. kosher salt
- 1/4 C. honey
- 4 boneless skinless chicken breast halves
- 1/4 C. buttermilk
- 1 C. all-purpose flour
- 1 tsp black pepper
- 1/2 tsp garlic salt
- 1/2 tsp onion salt
- cayenne pepper to taste
- vegetable oil for frying

Directions

1. Get a bowl, combine: honey, water, and salt.
2. Stir the mix for a few mins then add in your chicken and place everything in the fridge for 60 mins covered.
3. Then drain the liquid.
4. Add in your buttermilk and let the chicken sit in the milk for 20 mins.
5. Get a 2nd bowl, add: cayenne, flour, onion salt, black pepper, and garlic salt.
6. Dredge the chicken in the flour and then place them in on a wire rack for 20 mins.
7. Get your veggie oil hot then fry the chicken in it for 16 mins. Ensure that the internal temperature of the chicken is 165 before serving.
8. Let the chicken cool for 10 mins.
9. Enjoy.

RESTAURANT STYLE
Chicken II

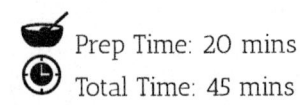

Prep Time: 20 mins
Total Time: 45 mins

Servings per Recipe: 2
Calories   390 kcal
Fat   10.8 g
Carbohydrates   13.3g
Protein   57.4 g
Cholesterol   1147 mg
Sodium   581 mg

Ingredients

2 large skinless, boneless chicken breast halves
salt and black pepper to taste
8 asparagus spears, trimmed - divided
1/2 C. shredded mozzarella cheese, divided
1/4 C. Italian seasoned bread crumbs

Directions

1. Coat a casserole dish with oil or nonstick spray and then set your oven to 375 degrees before doing anything else.
2. With a mallet pound out your chicken breast on a working surface then top everything with pepper and salt.
3. Put 4 pieces of asparagus in the middle of each, then a quarter of a C. of cheese.
4. Shape the chicken into rolls then layer them in the casserole dish with the seam portion facing downwards.
5. Top each one with 2 tbsps of bread crumbs.
6. Cook everything in the oven for 30 mins.
7. Enjoy.

Artisan Style Chicken with Artichokes

Prep Time: 20 mins
Total Time: 40 mins

Servings per Recipe: 6
Calories	408 kcal
Fat	18.6 g
Carbohydrates	22g
Protein	40.1 g
Cholesterol	98 mg
Sodium	719 mg

Ingredients

- 1 C. whole wheat or white flour
- 1/2 tsp salt
- 1/8 tsp white pepper, or to taste
- 1/8 tsp black pepper, or to taste
- 2 lbs chicken breast tenderloins or strips
- 2 tbsps canola oil
- 2 tbsps extra-virgin olive oil
- 2 C. chicken broth
- 2 tbsps fresh lemon juice
- 1 (12 oz.) jar quartered marinated artichoke hearts, with liquid
- 1/4 C. capers
- 2 tbsps butter
- 1/4 C. chopped flat-leaf parsley

Directions

1. Get a bowl, mix: black pepper, flour, white pepper, and salt.
2. Coat your chicken with the flour mix then fry them in olive and canola oil until fully done. Then place to the side.
3. Now pour in lemon juice and broth then get it simmering and then add in the capers and artichokes.
4. Get it simmering again.
5. Continue to simmer with a low level of heat until half of the liquid has evaporated.
6. Add the butter into the mix and let it melt before adding back in the chicken and simmering for 3 mins.
7. Serve the chicken with some parsley and a liberal amount of sauce.
8. Enjoy.

CHICKEN
Chili II

Prep Time: 20 mins
Total Time: 3 hrs 20 mins

Servings per Recipe: 4
Calories   199 kcal
Fat   8.3 g
Carbohydrates   2.1g
Protein   27.6 g
Cholesterol   79 mg
Sodium   259 mg

Ingredients

- 1/2 C. shredded Cheddar cheese
- 1/4 C. chopped green bell pepper
- 1/4 C. chopped red bell pepper
- 1/4 C. minced cilantro
- 1/4 C. diced tomatoes
- 1/2 tsp chili powder
- 1/2 tsp ground cumin
- 1/8 tsp salt
- 4 skinless, boneless chicken breast halves - flattened
- toothpicks

Directions

1. Get a bowl, combine: salt, tomatoes, cumin, cheddar, chili powder, cilantro, red and green peppers.
2. Dip your chicken breasts in the mix and then roll them up.
3. Place a toothpick in each piece of chicken and put the rolls in the slow cooker.
4. Add the rest of the mix to the slow cooker and then cook everything for 90 mins with high heat.
5. Enjoy.

Goat Cheese and Balsamic Chicken Breast

Prep Time: 15 mins
Total Time: 45 mins

Servings per Recipe: 2
Calories   340 kcal
Fat   13.5 g
Carbohydrates   23.5g
Protein   30.1 g
Cholesterol   83 mg
Sodium   230 mg

Ingredients

- 1 tsp olive oil
- 1 shallot, finely diced
- 1 C. balsamic vinegar
- 2 skinless, boneless chicken breast halves
- 2 oz. goat cheese, divided

Directions

1. Set your oven to 350 degrees before doing anything else.
2. Stir fry your shallots in olive oil for 7 mins then add in the balsamic and cook for 12 mins while stirring with a low heat and a gentle boil.
3. With a mallet flatten your chicken pieces then add: half of the cheese, and 1/3 of the balsamic mix.
4. Roll up the chicken pieces around the mix and then stake a toothpick through each before layering them all in a casserole dish.
5. Pour the rest of the balsamic over the chicken in the dish and then cook everything in the oven for 40 mins.
6. Enjoy.

CREOLE STYLE
Chicken I

🍲 Prep Time: 15 mins
🕐 Total Time: 5 hrs 35 mins

Servings per Recipe: 8
Calories   389 kcal
Fat   19.2 g
Carbohydrates   27.9 g
Protein   24.5 g
Cholesterol   81 mg
Sodium   1083 mg

Ingredients

8 chicken thighs
1/4 lb cooked turkey bacon, cut into one inch cubes
1 (16 oz.) can diced tomatoes
1 green bell pepper, chopped
6 green onions, chopped
1 (6 oz.) can tomato paste
1 tsp salt
2 dashes hot pepper sauce
2 C. water
1 C. uncooked long grain white rice
1/2 lb Polish beef sausage, sliced diagonally

Directions

1. Put the following in your crock pot: hot sauce, chicken, salt, turkey bacon, tomato paste, tomatoes, onions, and bell peppers.
2. Place a lid on the slow cooker and with low heat let the contents cook for 5 hrs.
3. Get your rice and water boiling then place a lid on the pot, set the heat to low, and let it cook for 22 mins.
4. Add the sausage and the rice to the crock pot and continue cooking for 40 mins with a high level of heat. At this point the sausage should be completely done.
5. Enjoy.

Thai Style Chicken III

Prep Time: 15 mins
Total Time: 8 hrs 15 mins

Servings per Recipe: 4
Calories	562 kcal
Fat	35.9 g
Carbohydrates	13.7g
Protein	47.6 g
Cholesterol	137 mg
Sodium	860 mg

Ingredients

- 3/4 C. hot salsa
- 1/4 C. chunky peanut butter
- 3/4 C. light coconut milk
- 2 tbsps lime juice
- 1 tbsp soy sauce
- 1 tsp white sugar
- 2 tbsps grated fresh ginger
- 2 lbs skinless chicken thighs
- 1/2 C. chopped peanuts, for topping
- 2 tbsps chopped cilantro, for topping

Directions

1. Add the following to your slow cooker: ginger, salsa, sugar, peanut butter, soy sauce, coconut milk, and lime juice.
2. Add in the chicken as well and cook everything for 9 hours with a low level of heat.
3. When serving the chicken add a topping of cilantro and peanuts.
4. Enjoy.

CHILI PEPPERS and Monterey Chicken (Mexican Style)

Prep Time: 30 mins
Total Time: 4 hrs 30 mins

Servings per Recipe: 10
Calories	824 kcal
Fat	44 g
Carbohydrates	66.4g
Protein	40 g
Cholesterol	123 mg
Sodium	1931 mg

Ingredients

15 boneless, skinless chicken thighs
1 (26 oz.) can condensed cream of chicken soup
2 cloves garlic, chopped (optional)
1 (16 oz.) container sour cream
1 (7 oz.) can diced green chili peppers
15 flour tortillas
3 1/2 C. shredded Monterey Jack cheese
1 (10 oz.) can sliced black olives (optional)
chives for garnish (optional)
black pepper to taste

Directions

1. Boil your chicken in water for 12 mins. Then remove all the liquid and chunk the chicken when it is cool enough.
2. Place everything into a bowl.
3. Add to the chicken: chilies, soup, sour cream, and garlic.
4. Coat your crock pot with nonstick spray then layer pieces of ripped tortillas at the bottom. Now layer half of the chicken mix, half of cheese, and then the soup over the tortillas.
5. Continue layering until all of ingredients have been used up.
6. Now add a final layering of olives.
7. Cook the contents with a low level of heat for 5 hours.
8. Enjoy.

Vinegar and Salt Chicken (English Style)

Prep Time: 15 mins
Total Time: 2 hrs

Servings per Recipe: 8
Calories	418 kcal
Fat	37.6 g
Carbohydrates	0.7g
Protein	16.6 g
Cholesterol	82 mg
Sodium	937 mg

Ingredients

- 2 C. cider vinegar
- 1 C. vegetable oil
- 1 egg, lightly beaten
- 3 tsps salt
- 1 tsp poultry seasoning
- 8 boneless chicken thighs, with skin

Directions

1. Get a bowl, combine: poultry seasoning, chicken, vinegar, salt, veggie oil, and beaten eggs.
2. Stir everything to coat the chicken and then place a covering of plastic on the bowl and let it sit in the fridge for 2 hrs.
3. Set your oven to 350 degrees before doing anything else.
4. Layer your chicken pieces in a casserole dish and top them with half of the marinade.
5. Cook everything in the oven for 35 mins then remove any liquids.
6. Now cook for 17 more mins until the chicken is fully done and a bit crispy.
7. Enjoy.

ARABIC STYLE
Chicken

🥣 Prep Time: 10 mins
🕐 Total Time: 45 mins

Servings per Recipe: 6
Calories 331 kcal
Fat 19.7 g
Carbohydrates 3.6g
Protein 29.8 g
Cholesterol 106 mg
Sodium 95 mg

Ingredients

1 tsp olive oil
1 C. sliced onion
2 1/2 lbs skinless, boneless chicken thighs
1 tbsp garam masala
1/2 tsp curry powder
1/2 C. beef broth
2 tbsps apple cider vinegar
1 C. fat-free, reduced-sodium chicken broth

Directions

1. Stir fry your onions in olive oil for 9 mins then place them to the side.
2. Turn up the heat and top your chicken with some curry and masala before laying it in the pan and browning it for 5 mins.
3. Now flip the chicken and cook it for 5 more mins.
4. Add in the broth and vinegar and cook for 2 mins before scraping the bottom of the pan.
5. Add the broth and onions and get everything boiling.
6. Once it is boiling place a lid on the pot, set the heat to low, and let the contents gently simmer for 22 mins.
7. Enjoy.

Parsley, Peppers, and Sweet Onions Chicken

- Prep Time: 10 mins
- Total Time: 1 hr 10 mins

Servings per Recipe: 4
Calories	420 kcal
Fat	18.6 g
Carbohydrates	22.1g
Protein	42.2 g
Cholesterol	114 mg
Sodium	163 mg

Ingredients

- 3 tbsps vegetable oil
- 2 red bell peppers, seeded and diced
- 2 large sweet onions, peeled and cut into wedges
- 1 1/2 lbs skinless, boneless chicken boneless thighs - cut into cubes
- 2 cloves garlic, minced
- 1 pinch ground cayenne pepper
- 1 lemon, juiced
- 2 tbsps butter
- 2 tbsps chopped fresh parsley
- salt and pepper to taste

Directions

1. Stir fry your onions and bell peppers in oil until tender then place them to the side.
2. Combine the chicken into the pan and brown them before adding the red pepper and garlic.
3. Cook for 3 mins with a low heat then add in lemon juice and scrape the bottom of the pan.
4. Combine in your butter and let it melt.
5. Now add the pepper mix back into the pan as well.
6. Cook for about 4 more mins before topping with parsley and some pepper and salt.
7. Enjoy.

AFRICAN STYLE
Chicken

Prep Time: 10 mins
Total Time: 1 hr 20 mins

Servings per Recipe: 6
Calories 495 kcal
Fat 29 g
Carbohydrates 25g
Protein 33.5 g
Cholesterol 158 mg
Sodium 566 mg

Ingredients

12 chicken thighs
1 (12 oz.) jar hot chutney
1 (1 oz.) package dry onion soup mix

Directions

1. Set your oven to 375 degrees before doing anything else.
2. Get a bowl, combine: soup and chutney.
3. Top your chicken with some pepper and salt and lay them into a casserole dish.
4. Top the chicken pieces with your wet mix and cook them in the oven for 65 mins.
5. Baste the chicken at least once with any drippings
6. Enjoy.

Japanese Style Chicken III

🥣 Prep Time: 15 mins
🕐 Total Time: 40 mins

Servings per Recipe: 4
Calories	688 kcal
Fat	14.6 g
Carbohydrates	97.9g
Protein	35.3 g
Cholesterol	208 mg
Sodium	1226 mg

Ingredients

- 2 C. uncooked jasmine rice
- 4 C. water
- 4 skinless, boneless chicken thighs, cut into small pieces
- 1 onion, cut in half and sliced
- 2 C. dashi stock, made with dashi powder
- 1/4 C. soy sauce
- 3 tbsps white vinegar
- 3 tbsps brown sugar
- 4 eggs

Directions

1. Run your rice under water then add them to 4 C. of fresh water in a pot and get it boiling.
2. Once everything is boiling place a lid on the pot, set the heat to low, and let the contents simmer for 22 mins.
3. Get a pan and coat it with nonstick spray.
4. Cook your chicken until fully done, in the pan, while covered, for 7 mins, then add the onions and cook for 7 more mins.
5. Add in the following: sugar, stock, white vinegar, and soy sauce.
6. Get the mixture boiling while stirring and then let it thicken for about 9 to 12 mins.
7. Beat your eggs and then add them to the stock.
8. Place a lid on the pan and set the heat to low. Let the eggs poach for 7 mins or until cooked.
9. Now shut the heat.
10. Get a bowl for serving and add some rice, 1/4 of the chicken mix, and half a C. of soup.
11. Enjoy.

CRANBERRIES and Onions Chicken

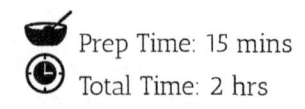

Prep Time: 15 mins
Total Time: 2 hrs

Servings per Recipe: 7
Calories   397 kcal
Fat   20.8 g
Carbohydrates   38.4g
Protein   15 g
Cholesterol   68 mg
Sodium   828 mg

Ingredients

6 chicken thighs
1 (8 oz.) bottle Russian-style salad dressing
1 (16 oz.) can cranberry sauce
1 packet dry onion soup mix

Directions

1. Set your oven to 350 degrees before doing anything else.
2. Get a bowl, combine: soup mix, dressing, and cranberry sauce.
3. Coat a casserole dish with nonstick spray and layer your chicken pieces in it. Cover the chicken with the wet mix.
4. Place some foil around the casserole dish and cook it in the oven for 90 mins.
5. When 20 mins is left take off the foil and finish the baking.
6. Enjoy.

Creamy Chipotle Chicken

Prep Time: 5 mins
Total Time: 55 mins

Servings per Recipe: 8
Calories	362 kcal
Fat	23.6 g
Carbohydrates	3.9 g
Protein	31.7 g
Cholesterol	119 mg
Sodium	589 mg

Ingredients

- 8 chicken leg quarters
- 1 1/2 C. milk
- 1 C. sour cream
- 2 chipotle peppers in adobo sauce
- 2 tbsps chicken bouillon granules
- 1 tbsp margarine
- salt to taste

Directions

1. Set your oven to 375 degrees F before doing anything else.
2. Arrange the chicken legs in a greased roasting pan and cook in the oven for about 30-40 minutes or till done completely.
3. Meanwhile in a blender, add the remaining ingredients except margarine and salt and pulse till smooth.
4. In a large pan, melt margarine on medium heat and stir in the chipotle mixture.
5. Bring to a gentle simmer and reduce the heat to low.
6. Stir in roasted chicken legs and salt and simmer for about 10 minutes or till chicken is well combined with the flavors of sauce.

SWEET & SPICY Mustard Chicken Thighs

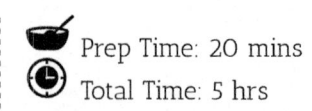

Prep Time: 20 mins
Total Time: 5 hrs

Servings per Recipe: 8
Calories   352 kcal
Fat   19 g
Carbohydrates   13.8g
Protein   29.1 g
Cholesterol   106 mg
Sodium   765 mg

Ingredients

8 large bone-in, skin-on chicken thighs
1/2 C. Dijon mustard
1/4 C. packed brown sugar
1/4 C. apple cider vinegar
1 tsp dry mustard powder
1 tsp salt
1 tsp freshly ground black pepper
1/2 tsp ground dried chipotle pepper
1 pinch cayenne pepper, or to taste
4 cloves garlic, minced
1 onion, sliced into rings
2 tsps vegetable oil, or as needed

Directions

1. With a sharp knife, cut 2 (1-inch apart) slashes into the skin and meat to the bone of the chicken thighs crosswise.
2. In a large bowl, mix together all the ingredients except onion and oil and transfer the mixture into a large resealable bag.
3. Add the chicken thighs and shake the bag to coat with marinade evenly and seal the bag tightly.
4. Refrigerate to marinate for about 4-8 hours.
5. Set your oven to 450 degrees F before doing anything else and line a large baking sheet with a lightly greased piece of foil.
6. Spread the onion rings onto the prepared baking sheet evenly and top with chicken thighs.
7. Coat the thighs with oil and sprinkle with seasoning if you like.
8. Cook in the oven for about 35-45 minutes or till done completely.
9. In a large serving platter, place thighs and onion rings.
10. In a small pan, add the baking sheet drippings and cook, stirring occasionally for about 3-4 minutes or till it reduces to half.
11. Serve the chicken and onion rings with the topping of pan sauce.

Chicken in Chipotle Gravy

Prep Time: 5 mins
Total Time: 20 mins

Servings per Recipe: 2
Calories	333 kcal
Fat	22.2 g
Carbohydrates	4.1g
Protein	28.3 g
Cholesterol	104 mg
Sodium	188 mg

Ingredients

2 skinless, boneless chicken breast halves
salt and fresh ground pepper to taste
1 tbsp olive oil
2 tbsps butter
1 tbsp all-purpose flour
3/4 C. chicken broth
2 tbsps minced green onions
1/2 tsp chipotle chili powder, or more to taste

Directions

1. With a meat mallet, pound the chicken breast halves into 1/2-inch thickness by it placing between 2 heavy plastic sheets.
2. In a skillet, heat the oil till it begins to simmer on high heat.
3. Reduce the heat to medium and add the chicken breasts and sprinkle with salt and black pepper.
4. Cook the chicken for about 5 minutes on both sides or till browned.
5. Place the breasts into a plate covered with foil to keep them warm.
6. In the same skillet melt the butter and cook the flour stirring continuously for about 2 minutes.
7. Add the broth and cook, scraping the brown bits for about 1-2 minutes.
8. Stir in the chicken, chipotle powder and green onion and cook for about 1-2 minutes.

CREAMY Chipotle Chicken Sandwich

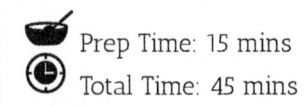

Prep Time: 15 mins
Total Time: 45 mins

Servings per Recipe: 4
Calories	451 kcal
Fat	17.3 g
Carbohydrates	35.2g
Protein	37.7 g
Cholesterol	92 mg
Sodium	757 mg

Ingredients

2 tsps olive oil
4 skinless, boneless chicken breast halves
1 tbsp apple cider vinegar
1 tbsp fresh lime juice
1/2 tsp white sugar
salt and ground black pepper to taste
1 green onion, chopped
1 clove garlic, minced
1/2 tsp dried oregano

1/3 C. light mayonnaise
1 tbsp canned chipotle peppers in adobo sauce, seeded and minced
1 1/2 tbsps chopped green onion
1 1/2 tbsps sweet pickle relish
8 slices sourdough bread
4 slices mozzarella cheese
1 C. torn lettuce

Directions

1. In a large skillet, heat the oil on medium heat and sear the chicken breasts for about 10 minutes per side or till browned.
2. Stir in 1 tsp lime juice, vinegar, garlic, green onion, sugar, oregano, salt and black pepper and cook for about 5 minutes per side.
3. Transfer the chicken mixture into a plate and cover with a piece of foil to keep warm.
4. In a blender, add chipotle pepper and mayonnaise and pulse till smooth.
5. In a bowl, mix together chipotle mayonnaise, sweet pickle relish and remaining green onion.
6. Toast the slices of bread.
7. Spread chipotle mayonnaise over 4 bread slices evenly.
8. Divide lettuce over the remaining 4 bread slices evenly, followed by 1 chicken breast and 1 cheese slice.
9. Cover with the slices of mayonnaise to make a sandwich and serve immediately.

Rosa's Latin Chowder

Prep Time: 20 mins
Total Time: 55 mins

Servings per Recipe: 8
Calories   367 kcal
Fat   21.3 g
Carbohydrates   15.1g
Protein   30 g
Cholesterol   109 mg
Sodium   868 mg

Ingredients

1 1/2 lb. boneless skinless chicken breasts cut into bite-size pieces
1/2 C. chopped onion
1 clove garlic, minced
3 tbsp butter
2 cubes chicken bouillon
1 C. hot water
3/4 tsp ground cumin
2 C. half-and-half cream
2 C. shredded Monterey Jack cheese
1 (14.75 oz.) can cream-style corn
1 (4 oz.) can diced green chilis
1 dash hot pepper sauce
1 tomato, chopped
Fresh cilantro sprigs, for garnish

Directions

1. In a Dutch oven, melt the butter on medium heat and cook the chicken, onion and garlic till the chicken is no longer pink.
2. In a bowl, dissolve the bouillon in hot water.
3. Add the bouillon mixture into the Dutch oven and stir to combine.
4. Stir in the cumin and bring to a boil.
5. Reduce the heat to low and simmer, covered for about 5 minutes.
6. Stir in the cream, cheese, corn, chilies and hot pepper sauce and simmer till the cheese is melted, stirring occasionally.
7. Stir in the chopped tomato and remove from the heat.
8. Serve with a garnishing of the cilantro.

CHICKEN Chowder for Champions

Prep Time: 20 mins
Total Time: 50 mins

Servings per Recipe: 5
Calories   691 kcal
Fat   41.3 g
Carbohydrates   35.7g
Protein   43.5 g
Cholesterol   126 mg
Sodium   2209 mg

Ingredients

4 C. chicken broth
1 1/2 C. diced potatoes
1 C. diced celery
1 C. diced carrots
1 C. diced onion
1/3 C. margarine
1/3 C. all-purpose flour

3 C. milk
1 tbsp soy sauce
1 lb. processed cheese, cubed
2 C. chopped, cooked chicken meat

Directions

1. In a large pan, mix together the chicken broth, potatoes, celery, carrots and onion and cook, covered for about 15 minutes.
2. In a medium pan, melt the butter on low heat.
3. Stir in the flour and cook for about 1 minute, stirring continuously.
4. Slowly, add the milk, beating continuously.
5. Cook till the mixture becomes thick and bubbly, stirring continuously.
6. Add the flour mixture and soy sauce into the vegetables and stir to combine.
7. Stir in the cheese till melts completely.
8. Stir in the chicken and cook till heated completely.

Grocery Store Rotisserie Chowder

⏲ Prep Time: 25 mins
🕐 Total Time: 1 hr 10 mins

Servings per Recipe: 8
Calories	443 kcal
Fat	22 g
Carbohydrates	49.9 g
Protein	15.2 g
Cholesterol	77 mg
Sodium	489 mg

Ingredients

- 1/2 C. butter
- 1 small carrot, finely diced
- 1 stalk celery, diced
- 1 small onion, finely diced
- 1 clove garlic, minced
- 1/2 C. all-purpose flour
- 1 1/2 C. white corn kernels
- 1 1/2 C. yellow corn kernels
- 4 russet potatoes, diced
- 2 cooked rotisserie chicken breast halves, shredded
- 4 C. chicken stock, divided
- 2 1/2 C. half-and-half
- 1 pinch allspice
- Salt and ground black pepper to taste

Directions

1. In a large pan, melt the butter on medium heat and sauté the carrot, celery, onion and garlic for about 2 minutes.
2. Stir in the flour and cook for about 5 minutes, stirring continuously.
3. Remove from the heat and keep aside to cool for about 15 minutes.
4. In a large pan, mix together the corn kernels, potatoes, chicken, and 3 C. of the chicken stock on medium heat.
5. Add remaining 1 C. of the chicken stock into the flour mixture and beat till well combined.
6. Add the flour mixture into the pan with the corn mixture and bring to a gentle boil, stirring continuously.
7. Boil for about 5 minutes, stirring continuously.
8. Stir in the half-and-half, allspice, salt and black pepper and bring to a boil.
9. Reduce the heat to low and simmer for about 20 minutes.

HOW TO
Roast a Chicken

Prep Time: 10 mins
Total Time: 1 hr 40 mins

Servings per Recipe: 6
Calories   423 kcal
Fat   32.1 g
Carbohydrates   1.2g
Protein   30.9 g
Cholesterol   97 mg
Sodium   662 mg

Ingredients

1 (3 lb) whole chicken, giblets removed
salt and black pepper to taste
1 tbsp onion powder, or to taste
1/2 C. margarine, divided
1 stalk celery, leaves removed

Directions

1. Before you do anything set the oven to 350 F.
2. Season the whole chicken with some salt and pepper. Season its inside with onion powder and place in it 3 tbsp of margarine.
3. Place the whole chicken in a large roasting pan and place the remaining margarine on it in the shape of dollops. Chop the celery into pieces and place them in the middle of the chicken.
4. Place the chicken in the oven and roast it for 1 h 20 min. Baste the chicken with the fat and melted margarine that pooled around whole cooking.
5. Place a large piece of foil over the chicken and allow it to rest for 35 min. Serve it warm.
6. Enjoy.

Fall-Spice Chicken Roast

Prep Time: 15 mins
Total Time: 1 d 1 h 35 m

Servings per Recipe: 6
Calories   387 kcal
Fat   22.8 g
Carbohydrates   1.6 g
Protein   41 g
Cholesterol   129 mg
Sodium   900 mg

Ingredients

- 2 tsp salt
- 1 tsp white sugar
- 1/8 tsp ground cloves
- 1/8 tsp ground allspice
- 1/8 tsp ground cinnamon
- 1 (4 lb) whole chicken
- 5 cloves garlic, crushed

Directions

1. Get a small mixing bowl: Mix in it the salt, sugar, cloves, allspice, and cinnamon to make the rub. Massage the rub into the chicken and place it in the fridge for a whole 24 h day.
2. Before you do anything set the oven to 500 F.
3. Place the garlic and inside of the chicken and place it with its breast facing down in a roasting pan.
4. Cook in the oven for 17 min. Lower the oven heat to 450 F and cook the chicken for another 17 min.
5. Baste the chicken with the fat and dripping that gathered in the roasting pan. Once again reduce the oven heat to 425 F and cook the chicken for 32 min.
6. Cover the chicken with a piece of foil and let it rest for 22 min then serve it.
7. Enjoy.

4-INGREDIENT
Chicken Roast

Prep Time: 10 mins
Total Time: 2 hrs 10 mins

Servings per Recipe: 6
Calories	291 kcal
Fat	17.2 g
Carbohydrates	1.3g
Protein	30.8 g
Cholesterol	97 mg
Sodium	94 mg

Ingredients

1 (3 lb) whole chicken, rinsed
salt and pepper to taste
1 small onion, quartered

1/4 C. chopped fresh rosemary

Directions

1. Before you do anything set the oven to 350 F.
2. Sprinkle some salt and pepper on the whole chicken then place the rosemary with onion in its cavity.
3. Place the chicken in a large roasting pan and cook it in the oven for 2 h 32 min. Allow the chicken to rest for 15 to 20 min then serve it.
4. Enjoy.

Southern Italian Chicken Roast

🥣 Prep Time: 15 mins
🕐 Total Time: 1 hr 45 mins

Servings per Recipe: 8
Calories   405 kcal
Fat   29.2 g
Carbohydrates   3.6g
Protein   32.2 g
Cholesterol   128 mg
Sodium   178 mg

Ingredients

- 2 tsp Italian seasoning
- 1/2 tsp seasoning salt
- 1/2 tsp mustard powder
- 1 tsp garlic powder
- 1/2 tsp ground black pepper
- 1 (3 lb) whole chicken
- 2 lemons
- 2 tbsp olive oil

Directions

1. Before you do anything set the oven to 350 F.
2. Get a small bowl: Mix in it the mustard powder with garlic powder, a pinch of salt and pepper to make the rub.
3. Massage the rub into the chicken from using 1 1/2 tsp for the inside and the remaining seasoning for the outside.
4. Get a small mixing bowl: Mix in it the olive oil with the juice of 2 lemons then pour it all over the chicken.
5. Roast the chicken in the oven for 1 h 32 min while basting it with the drippings from the pan every 30 min. Allow the roast to rest for 15 min then serve it.
6. Enjoy.

HERBS
Marinade for Chicken Roast

Prep Time: 10 mins
Total Time: 10 mins

Servings per Recipe: 4
Calories   20 kcal
Fat   0.3 g
Carbohydrates   4.4g
Protein   0.8 g
Cholesterol   0 mg
Sodium   977 mg

Ingredients

1 tbsp celery flakes
1 tbsp kosher salt
1 tbsp paprika
1 tbsp garlic powder
1 tbsp onion powder
1 tbsp ground thyme

2 tsp dried sage
1 1/2 tsp ground black pepper
1 1/2 tsp dried rosemary
1/2 tsp cayenne pepper

Directions

1. Get a small bowl: Combine it all the ingredients and whisk them well.
2. Get a food processor: Transfer the mix to it and blend them smooth. Massage the marinade with some olive oil to the chicken and roasted the way you like.
3. Enjoy.

Mediterranean Chicken Legs

Prep Time: 10 mins
Total Time: 1 hr 25 mins

Servings per Recipe: 4
Calories   516 kcal
Fat   34.6 g
Carbohydrates   16.8g
Protein   41.9 g
Cholesterol   140 mg
Sodium   2464 mg

Ingredients

- 4 chicken leg quarters, with bone and skin
- 1/4 C. olive oil
- 4 lemons, halved
- 4 tsp dried oregano
- 4 tsp dried basil
- 4 tsp garlic powder
- 4 tsp salt
- 4 tsp ground black pepper

Directions

1. Before you do anything set the oven to 350 F.
2. Coat each chicken quarter with 1 tbsp of olive oil then drizzle the lemon juice of 2 lemons all over them.
3. Place the chicken quarters in a large roasting pan and put the lemon halves beside them.
4. Get a small mixing bowl: Mix in it the oregano with garlic powder, basil, a pinch of salt and pepper then sprinkle the mix all over the chicken legs equally.
5. Roast the chicken legs for 1 h 20 min while basting them with the drippings every once in a while then serve them warm.
6. Enjoy.

GREEK INSPIRED
Chicken Roast

Prep Time: 15 mins
Total Time: 1 hr

Servings per Recipe: 6
Calories	546 kcal
Fat	34.5 g
Carbohydrates	5.4g
Protein	52 g
Cholesterol	205 mg
Sodium	347 mg

Ingredients

- 1 whole chicken, cut into 8 pieces
- 1 onion, cut into wedges
- 1 lemon, sliced
- 8 cloves garlic
- 4 sprigs fresh rosemary
- 1/4 C. olive oil
- 1/2 tsp salt
- 1/2 tsp ground black pepper

Directions

1. Before you do anything set the oven to 450 F.
2. Get a large bowl: Stir in the lemon slices with garlic, rosemary, chicken and onion then pour the oil all over them and stir them.
3. Season them with some salt and pepper then stir them again.
4. Lay the chicken pieces in a large roasting pan and cook them for 48 min. Allow them to rest for 10 min then serve them warm.
5. Enjoy.

Glazed Chicken Roast

🥣 Prep Time: 15 mins
⏱ Total Time: 1 hr 55 mins

Servings per Recipe: 6
Calories   469 kcal
Fat   26 g
Carbohydrates   10g
Protein   46.4 g
Cholesterol   145 mg
Sodium   836 mg

Ingredients

2 (3 lb) whole chickens, quartered
Chicken Spice Rub:
1 tbsp brown sugar
1 tbsp sea salt
1 1/2 tsp garlic powder
1 1/2 tsp onion powder
1 1/2 tsp paprika
1 tsp dried oregano
1/2 tsp dry mustard
1/2 tsp celery seed
1/4 tsp cayenne pepper

Glaze:
1/4 C. maple syrup
1 tbsp yellow mustard
1 1/2 tsp spicy brown mustard
1/2 tsp garlic powder
1/2 tsp onion powder
1/2 tsp paprika
1/4 tsp ground black pepper

Directions

1. Get a small bowl: Mix in it the sugar, sea salt, 1 1/2 tsp garlic powder, 1 1/2 tsp onion powder, 1 1/2 tsp paprika, oregano, dry mustard, celery seed, and cayenne pepper.
2. Massage the spices mix into the chicken pieces and place them in a plastic wrap and place them in the fridge for 1 h to absorb the flavors.
3. To make the glaze: Get a small bowl and mix in it the maple syrup, yellow mustard, brown mustard, 1/2 tsp garlic powder, 1/2 tsp onion powder, 1/2 tsp paprika, and black pepper.
4. Before you do anything set the oven to 425 F.
5. Place the breasts pieces in the middles and place the remaining chicken pieces on the sides then cook them in the oven for 17 min.
6. Brush the chicken pieces with the glaze then cook them for another 17 min. Brush the chicken pieces again and cook them for 12 to 14 min or until it the chicken is done.
7. Serve your roasted glazed chicken. Enjoy.

ORANGY
Baked Chicken

Prep Time: 10 mins
Total Time: 1 d 2 h 30 m

Servings per Recipe: 6
Calories 161 kcal
Fat 6.4 g
Carbohydrates 0.3g
Protein 24 g
Cholesterol 72 mg
Sodium 1816 mg

Ingredients

1 whole chicken
2 tbsp salt, or as needed
2 tsp grated orange zest
1 tsp dried rosemary
1 tsp dried thyme

Directions

1. Before you do anything set the oven to 350 F.
2. Get a small bowl: Mix in it the orange zest, rosemary, and thyme . Massage 3/4 of the mix into the chicken then place the remaining of it in the inside of the chicken.
3. Place a loose cover of plastic cover over the chicken then place in the fridge for 2 to days.
4. Place the chicken in a large roasting pan then cook it in the oven for 2 h 25 min. Place a sheet of foil over the chicken and place it aside to rest for 23 min then serve it.
5. Enjoy.

Baked Golden Chicken and Potato

Prep Time: 30 mins
Total Time: 1 hr 40 mins

Servings per Recipe: 6
Calories	423 kcal
Fat	18.9 g
Carbohydrates	33.8g
Protein	28.7 g
Cholesterol	81 mg
Sodium	161 mg

Ingredients

- 1 serving cooking spray
- 2 sweet potatoes, sliced very thinly
- 2 Yukon Gold potatoes, sliced
- 1 large onion, sliced
- 1 (2 to 3 lb) roasting chicken
- 2 tbsp olive oil, or to taste
- 1 pinch salt and ground black pepper to taste

Directions

1. Before you do anything set the oven to 400 F. Spray some cooking spray on a roasting pan and place it aside.
2. Place the sweet potato slices followed by golden potato and onion in the roasting pan.
3. Put the chicken on top with its breast facing down. Make a large cut alone the chicken backbone and remove it then press it open in the shape of a butterfly.
4. Drizzle the olive oil on the chicken and sprinkle on it some salt and pepper then place it with the breast facing down on the veggies.
5. Cook the chicken and potato in the oven for 1 h 10 min. Allow the potato and chicken roast to rest for 12 min then serve them warm.
6. Enjoy.

COUNTRY Chicken Roast Gravy

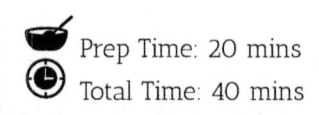

Prep Time: 20 mins
Total Time: 40 mins

Servings per Recipe: 20
Calories   43 kcal
Fat   0.4 g
Carbohydrates   4.2g
Protein   5.8 g
Cholesterol   < 1 mg
Sodium   464 mg

Ingredients

- 1/4 C. drippings from a roast chicken
- 2 C. cold chicken stock, or more if needed
- 2 1/2 tbsp all-purpose flour
- salt and ground black pepper to taste

Directions

1. Drain the fats from the dripping of a chicken roast pan and place it aside. Add the flour to the pan and mix it well then add some of the fat if the mix is too dry.
2. Transfer the flour mix to a small saucepan over low heat and cook it until it becomes light brown in color for about 6 min.
3. Stir in 1/3 C. of stock into the mix while mixing all the time then keep repeating the process with the remaining stock until you add all of it
4. Cook the gravy until it starts simmering then keep cooking it for 9 min until it becomes creamy and thick.
5. Pour the grave through a fine sieve and strain then pour it back into the saucepan and heat it through then serve it warm.
6. Enjoy.

Hot and Sweet Chicken Roast

Prep Time: 15 mins
Total Time: 1 hr 25 mins

Servings per Recipe: 6
Calories   558 kcal
Fat   26.8 g
Carbohydrates   37.1g
Protein   41.2 g
Cholesterol   140 mg
Sodium   225 mg

Ingredients

1 (4 lb) whole chicken, cut lengthwise
kosher salt to taste
freshly ground black pepper
1 tsp ground cinnamon, or as needed
1 C. water
1 C. maple syrup
1 lemon, juiced
2 chile peppers, chopped
2 tbsp butter, melted

Directions

1. Before you do anything set the oven to 375 F.
2. Season the chicken with cinnamon, salt and pepper. Pour the water in a broiler pan and place the chicken in it then cook it for 35 min.
3. Get a small bowl: Mix in it the maple syrup, lemon juice, and chile peppers. Pour the mix all over the chicken and cook it for 38 min.
4. Drain the chicken from the drippings and lay on it the butter then roast it in the oven for 14 min. Serve it warm.
5. Enjoy.

Printed in Great Britain
by Amazon